It Could Have Been a Hound

Published by Denny Publishing Limited
6 Cotswold Buisness Village
Moreton-in Marsh
Gloucestershire
GL56 0JQ
United Kingdom

First published October 2000

Set in 12/15 Rotis-Serif

A catalogue record for this book is avaliable from the British Library.

Printed by St Edmundsbury Press, Bury St Edmunds, Suffolk

ISBN: 1-903680-01-8

It Could Have Been a Hound

(and other stories)

Hunting with Ronnie Wallace

Compiled and edited by John Dorman
Illustrated by Gary Drew

DENNY PUBLISHING

Introduction

Had it been possible to talk to everyone who has a story to tell about Ronnie Wallace, this book would have taken years to compile and would probably have run to several volumes. However, in order to meet publishing deadlines it was necessary to have a cut-off point, and to all those who feel that they could – or should – have been asked to contribute, my apologies. To those whose stories appear on the following pages, and who are listed below, my grateful thanks.

John Dorman
July 2000

Anthony Adams, Huntsman, Heythrop
Ian Alexander, Heythrop
Rob Bartlett, Heythrop
Clem Barton
Di Barton
Caroline Brooks, Heythrop
Michael Clayton
Tom Clifford
Tony Collins, ex-huntsman, Heythrop
Robin Dale, Heythrop
Roger Dancer, Heythrop
John Gill, Heythrop
Sally Gill, Heythrop
Alistair Jackson, Director, MFHA
Stephen Lambert, Heythrop
Bill Lander, ex-Huntsman, Heythrop
John Lloyd, Heythrop
Sandra Loder, Heythrop
Peter Pauling, Heythrop
Nigel Peel, Jt. Master, North Cotswold
Celia Plunkett, Heythrop
John Robbins, Heythrop
George Smith, Heythrop
Derek Strong, Exmoor
Mary Studd, Heythrop

Richard Sumner, Jt Master, Heythrop
Robin Watson, Exmoor
Anthony Welton, Chairman, Heythrop
Lady Mary Rose Williams
John Wills, Jt. Master, Heythrop
Liz Wills, Heythrop
Tony Wright, Huntsman, Exmoor
Daphne Flowers Wood, Live Oak Hounds, Florida
Marty Wood, Live Oak Hounds, Florida

‘ You must take trouble. You musn't leave anything to chance —nothing to chance. ’

Captain Ronnie Wallace

‘ I was brought up to understand that you never, ever, rode past the Master or the Huntsman. We were over by the Rollrights near Chipping Norton one lovely sunny day, with the ground just right. The fox had gone away and the hounds were after it. I'd been a bit delayed so the bulk of the field was in front of me. I set off after them, and suddenly shot past Ronnie.

I immediately pulled my horse up and he came alongside me.

"I'm terribly sorry about that, Master", I said.

"Dear boy", he replied, "gallop on, and enjoy yourself!"

So I did. The hounds were way in front, then they checked, and who should be there but Ronnie. We'd been galloping all over the country behind the hounds, but of course he knew his way around so well that he knew exactly were the fox would be.

"Had a nice ride?", he asked me. ’

Ian Alexander

8

' Once, when I was scouting, I went up a valley with the hounds running, just to see the fox on. All good horses know where a fox goes: if you're scouting you might look one way and the horse the other, and he'll always prick his ears or move his head, which signals to you.

On this occasion I hadn't seen anything, but the horse had moved its head, and when the Master came up with the hounds I said, "I think the fox has gone left-handed."

The Captain replied, "Your job is not to think. Your job is to see the fox away and let me know. If there's any thinking to be done I'm going to do it." '

John Robbins

‘ I had a lurcher which was my favourite dog. Once, chasing a fox,
the fox went under a gate and the lurcher jumped the gate, land-
ing on top of the fox and killing it.

I thought this was a pretty impressive performance, and I was
sure no–one else could have seen it, but Ronnie rang me up about
it a few days later, and as a result I was forced to take on the
chairmanship of the Hunt Supporters' Club. ’

John Lloyd

‘ There was a character called John Birtles, who was rather eccentric
and quite cheeky. Ronnie was slightly irritated by him, but in an
odd way he also found him rather amusing.

Birtles turned up one day with rather long hair, and Ronnie had a
go at him.

"Get your bloody hair cut!", he barked.

"Yes sergeant!", Birtles shouted back, coming to attention. ’

Anthony Welton

10

❛ There was always something to be learnt from what he said. ❜

Stephen Lambert

❛ When the foot and mouth scare was on during the early 1970's we were off work for about eight weeks, which was very frustrating. During this time Bill Lander rang me one evening and said, "Meet me at the Bridges tomorrow morning," I met him, we went to Cornbury Park with the hounds, found a fox and killed it. Then we went home quietly and didn't tell anyone what we'd been up to.

That night the Captain rang Bill and said, "I hear you let the hounds get away from you this morning."

"Yes sir", Bill admitted, "we did."

"Don't let it happen again", the Captain told him.

And that was all. I don't know how, but he knew what we'd been doing! ❜

Roger Dancer

'We were in Warwickshire country one day and Ronnie was riding Bertha, a wonderful mare. She didn't go much faster than a trot, but she kept going.

I saw him heading towards a gate that was next to a humpbacked bridge, and I thought he was going straight for the gate. But instead, he trotted up onto the top of the bridge and jumped right over the gate from there. He wouldn't have done that on anything else but Bertha. '

Rob Bartlett

'I think the worst moment I had with him was when he got off his horse once to draw a cover. I was holding his horse and I brought it round, and both our horses were jiggling. I held the stirrup leather as he got on, and just as he did so the leather fell off the back of the saddle.

So I jumped off and tried to put it back on, he was on board, the hounds were running fast, and there was I trying to sort it all out. It was not easy. The air was very blue. '

Richard Sumner

6 Many times I have watched him cast his hounds and thought he would surely draw blank, but nine times out of ten he was right. His instinct for hunting was exceptional, and it was this that set him apart from other huntsmen. 9

Peter Pauling

6 In January 1975 I'd gone to a meet at Naunton Manor. We found a fox within two hundred yeards of the meet and we ran from Lower Slaughter through Swell, Stow, Maugersbury and Icomb to Bledington, where we came round the village and back up to Maugersbury again. We'd been riding hard and most of us had jumped anything between fifty and sixty fences.

The fox went into cover, the hounds went in and the fox was killed, and at that point the Captain just trotted up. He'd probably jumped no more than three or four fences and wouldn't have been in a bad hurry all the way. 9

Robin Dale

13

At the end of a day on Exmoor I got into the hunt lorry to drive to the kennels and the Captain came with me. We were crossing a very narrow bridge and he said, "Plenty of room on my side", so I moved over a little.

There was a crash as we hit the bridge parapet. The Captain had forgotten that the cab was quite a bit narrower than the back of the lorry.

John Robbins

He could be very formidable at times, but he was a very fair man; a good boss. I have a lot of respect for him.

Anthony Adams

14

He liked to do quite a lot of footwork, and the great skill when you were out hunting with him was to avoid having to lead his horse. I was doing this on Exmoor once, and the horse became stuck in a bog. A colleague and I struggled for over an hour to free it, while Ronnie sat under the only tree on Exmoor, issuing instructions.

Eventually we got it out, and we were exhausted and covered in mud, and looking forward to a hot bath. But far from going straight home, as we might have expected, Ronnie said, "You won't mind if we visit one or two farmers on the way back, will you?"

Stephen Lambert

He had an amateur whipper-in once, and every time he told him off this chap lifted his hat to him. One day Ronnie said, "Don't keep taking your hat off all the time — you'll catch cold."

"Rightho sir", the fellow replied, lifting his hat again.

Roger Dancer

'Clem Barton and I share the same birthday, April 5th, and we were out hunting on that day one year with the Exmoor. We had a very good hunt - although Clem fell in a bog - and I was riding a young horse of his which I hacked about ten miles home.

Clem's wife Di had prepared us a birthday tea which we tucked into, and after a while the great man came and joined us and we had a few glasses of whisky. Then he said, "I've brought you both a present."

We followed him out to his car in great anticipation, and he opened the boot and handed us the fox. It was dead, of course, and he wanted someone to bury it. '

Nigel Peel

16

' Tony Collins and I were with him one day, following the hounds down a particularly steep slope towards an enormous post-and-rail fence. The Captain seemed to be lining himself up for it, and we were both thinking "surely he's not going to try and jump that!"

At that point a lady member came hurtling through us totally out of control. She tore into the fence, took out the rails, and landed in the mud on the other side. In normal circumstances such an action would have resulted in a major roasting, but on this occasion the Captain just trotted through the gap and said, "Thank you madam, thank you. That's just what we wanted." '

Anthony Adams

‘ Cub-hunting at Farmington one day the hounds found the fox,
which went from one cover to another, although I hadn't seen it
go across. So when the Captain asked me if I'd seen it I said no.
Then it went left-handed round the village and up the other side,
and came out just above me on a hanging.

Once again the Captain said, "Clem, have you seen it? Where's it
gone?", but I still hadn't spotted it.

The Captain gave me a long look. "You're like a bloody fried egg
under a tree!", he said. ’

Clem Barton

‘ Towards the end of the Captain's time at the Heythrop four
members of the hunt got themselves into a position where they
shouldn't have been. They knew they'd cop it if the Captain saw
them, and when they spotted him approaching they locked themselves and their horses in a disused Nissen hut until he had moved
on, apparently unaware of their presence.

What they did not realise at the time was that the Captain not
only knew there were people in the Nissen hut, he also knew
exactly who they were. They were four very senior members of the
hunt, and very important people in their own right. What the
Captain said to them later is not recorded. ’

Anthony Adams/Tony Collins

18

Out hunting one day he turned round to the entire Heythrop field, which included at least one Duke and several other important people, and said, "Shut up, you bunch of half—wits; the hounds are out of touch!"

They had got a long way ahead, and he was listening for them.

Michael Clayton

When I was a young girl my father was Fieldmaster, and Ronnie often used to call at our house for tea. On more than one occasion he found me sobbing over my Latin prep, and he would peer over my shoulder and produce the answer. Sharpish.

Celia Plunkett

19

' We had had a lot of coughing in the yard, and I had just got a little grey horse back in action again, and I only wanted him ridden for half the day. We also had a big black horse with us which the Captain always hunted first.

I wanted him to ride the grey later in the day, but he wouldn't, and stayed on the black horse. It was nearly dusk when I saw him lolloping along towards a little rail, and I thought "I don't think that horse is going to make a very good job of that". I could see it was going to happen before it happened: it hit the top of the rail and tipped the Captain off.

I thought I was in for a rocket, but he just looked at me very sternly and said, "Take that horse and school the bloody thing!"

"That horse" had hunted two seasons with him and never put a foot wrong! '

Di Barton

20

❝ On the political side, the expression "walking the corridors of power" certainly applied to him. He made it his business to know all the right people and to nurture them, so he got the information he needed and could feed it back. He was a politician by nature. ❞

Alastair Jackson

❝ When I first started work with the Heythrop I was, as were most youngsters in the eyes of Captain Wallace, a silly boy. Sometimes I was a stupid boy, occasionally I was a stupid bloody fool and more often than not I was something far worse. But I had been warned that I would be shouted at a lot, and I tried to listen and learn from it, rather than let it upset me.

One morning the local builder, Mr. Sole, arrived at the kennels. The Captain had obviously arranged to meet him there, because as he walked through the stable yard he saw him and shouted out, "Ah, Sole!"

I thought at the time that Mr. Sole had got off rather lightly. ❞

Tony Wright

21

‘ If there was a big field on a Saturday Ronnie would sometimes move the hounds on if they lost the line of a particular fox. Most people didn't notice, but sometimes it caused confusion.

"Are we actually hunting?", I asked Richard Fleming on one occasion.

"Not necessarily", he replied. "I think you could say that we are moving forward with the option of finding a fresh fox." ’

John Gill

‘ Ronnie spotted Robert Warlock crossing a field of corn one day and summoned him over. He then proceeded to deliver a dressing down which must have lasted ten minutes. Robert took this and then returned to the rest of the field.

"Remarkable man", he commented. "He's got time to talk to everyone." ’

Sandra Loder

' We had come to a gate done up with string and I was told to cut it. I was fiddling about in my breeches pocket amongst the gloves and the Mars Bars and so on, and the Captain said, "Tony, always keep your knife in your ticket pocket: it's much easier to get at."

The same thing happened the following season, and I had the same problem, because my knife was a bit big for my ticket pocket, and awkward to get at.

"Tony", the Captain said, "always keep your knife in your breeches pocket: there's much more room in there." '

Tony Collins

23

' One day during a cracking hunt I saw a fox which had done a lot
of work come out onto the road. The Captain rode up and asked
me if I'd seen it, and I said, "Yes, it's gone down there. It's filthy
dirty."

He gave me a big roasting. "A hunted fox is never dirty", he told
me. "A hunted fox is always a clean fox."

The same thing happened a few days later, and when I told the
Captain I'd seen a fox he asked, "Was it a dirty fox that had done
a lot of work?"

"Yes", I told him.

"That's him!", the Captain said. '

Anthony Adams

' During the late 1960's I hunted with the Oakley, although I already
knew Ronnie Wallace through otter hunting, and he discovered I
had married a local farmer's daughter.

"Why don't you come and hunt with the Heythrop?", he asked
me.

I replied that I couldn't afford to buy a big chunk of land, which
was a requirement then.

"Oh, don't worry about that, dear boy", he said. "You've married
a farmer's daughter so you can hunt as a farmer's relative." '

Ian Alexander

The first time I went out with the Heythrop the Captain distributed the riders around the first covert and told me to come along with him. Hounds entered the covert, and then the Captain told me to wait on the other side of the wood and "to keep a tap on".

I hadn't the foggiest idea what he meant by this. I thought that perhaps I had to let one fox at a time leave the covert, as though turning a tap on and off. Luckily none of the foxes seemed to want to pass my way, and when I asked Tony Collins later what I should have been doing, he explained that I should tap the saddle flap with my whip hand to discourage any fox from leaving.

I realised then how close I had come to an early termination of my job.

Tony Wright

I've judged hounds with him, and he makes you feel you're contributing, even though he will more than likely have the final say. I remember one occasion when he had been rather well lunched, and in the afternoon had to judge a lot of almost white hounds.

"As far as I was concerned they were just like confetti", he said. "I couldn't tell one from the other."

He managed, however. He was the best judge of fox-hounds I've ever seen.

Michael Clayton

25

'What amazed me was the way the Captain ran the country; how he organised people to be in the right place at the right time, and the way he used the likes of Roger Dancer, Clem Barton, George Smith and John Robbins as scouts. They would go on and be five fields away, and if they saw a fox they just lifted their hats – no noise – so that he had a visual point and would draw his hounds on.

He knew exactly where the fox had gone through these scouts. They were extremely astute, clever, and in those days young farmers who worked with him as a team. '

Robin Dale

'Ronnie was a total professional and he expected everyone to follow the basic rules of hunting. Around the Slaughters one day the car followers kept heading the fox to the point where he had had enough.

He stopped the hounds, rode up to the cars and said, "As long as you continue to behave like this I'm taking the hounds home."

And he did, and quite right too. '

Ian Alexander

' Early one season the hounds were behaving very badly: in fact on one occasion there was a near-riot. Ronnie gathered them up and took them into a nearby building, while the rest of us waited outside in silence.

From inside the building came the sounds of a systematic ticking off, and the occasional wallopping. Those particular hounds never chased a hare again. '

John Gill

' Tony Wright once started a day's hunting on a young mare that had only recently been broken in. He intended to change horses later on.

He cantered up to the first covert and found he couldn't stop – the horse had run away with him – and he had to do a full swing round the field before he could pull up. Naturally the Captain saw this.

"Just because you've got two horses today", he said, "there's no need to go careering all over the country." '

Bill Lander

I've very rarely incurred the wrath of "God", but I remember one occasion when he told me to hold the field at the start of a meet while he went on to draw a cover. After a while, though, I edged up closer, whereupon the fox came out of the cover, through the hedge, and the hounds caught it right underneath my horse.

Ronnie appeared, speechless with rage.

"I told you", he said eventually. "I told you not to come any closer!"

All I could say was, "I'm really sorry". One of his main considerations on a day's hunting was to get a good start.

Robin Watson

There was a field of kale with set of rails at the bottom, and the top rail had been removed so that the field could get away quickly. Someone had suggested putting a gate there, but the Captain gave instructions to install only a narrow little gate, so that he could get away easily but the field would be held up.

George Smith

Once, when Colonel Taylor was Fieldmaster, I didn't go across one particular field, and the Captain wanted to know why.

"Because Colonel Taylor told me not to cross that field", I said.

"Don't take any notice of that silly old fool", the Captain told me. "You come with me."

But that night he said to me, "Forget what I said about Colonel Taylor today. He was one of the bravest men in the war.

Roger Dancer

One day we were up by Stow-on-the-Wold, and I was on one side of a valley and Ronnie was on the other. He suddenly started shouting that I shouldn't go any further, so I stopped and came back to his side of the valley, and sulked a bit and didn't go near him. Then he waved at me to come up to him.

"I'm sorry if I got a bit excited", he said.

"I don't mind, if I'm in the wrong", I told him.

"Well you're bloody well in the wrong now", he said, "so get forward and see if you can spot a fox."

Richard Sumner

'He once sent me home three times in one day. It was during one of my early years with the Heythrop — I was still in my teens and Ronnie was actually very good and encouraging to our age-group, even though he cursed us up and down hill!

On the evening in question my mother called me to the telephone and said that Captain Wallace wanted to speak to me. I was terrified; I thought it was the end of my hunting with the Heythrop.

"Did I send you home today?", he asked me.

"Yes, Captain Wallace", I replied, "you did, and I'm afraid I didn't go. In fact you sent me home another twice and I still didn't go."

"Oh good!", he said. "What a relief!" '

Anthony Welton

' I had recently bought a horse and was trying it out cub–hunting when it kicked out at John Ballard, the Secretary, and broke his leg. I was horrified, and wrote a note to Ronnie saying how sorry I was.

When I saw him a few days later he said to me, with a twinkle in his eye, "Don't take it to heart. It could have been far worse: it could have been a hound." '

Caroline Brooks

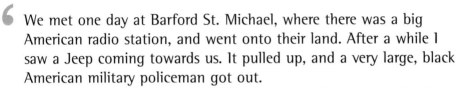

We met one day at Barford St. Michael, where there was a big American radio station, and went onto their land. After a while I saw a Jeep coming towards us. It pulled up, and a very large, black American military policeman got out.

"Get off this land straight away!", he ordered in a strong Yankee accent.

The Captain looked him straight in the eye.

"I don't like being ordered off a bit of England by an Englishman", he said, "and I'm buggered if I'm going to be ordered off it by a black American!"

Bill Lander

‘ One day, after we'd caught the fox, he came up to me and said, "Not a bad day apart from the fact that we had to go over your farm, John." He said that in front of everyone and I was so furious I let him have it back! ’

John Lloyd

‘ Towards the end of a day when there were not many of us left Ronnie disappeared into a covert with his hounds. Foxes came out heading in all directions but not a single hound, which was quite incredible.

Eventually there emerged a fox that was obviously going the way Ronnie wanted it, because the pack came streaming out of the covert behind it. We had a furious half hour round the Evenlode Vale before the fox was caught and killed in front of us. Then Ronnie just trotted up quietly, obviously pleased with the pack.

The fact that all the other foxes had been ignored was an amazing performance; certainly one that I have never seen matched anywhere else. ’

Michael Clayton

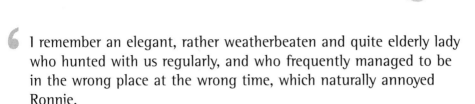

I remember an elegant, rather weatherbeaten and quite elderly lady who hunted with us regularly, and who frequently managed to be in the wrong place at the wrong time, which naturally annoyed Ronnie.

One day she came cantering right into the hounds, scattering them, and Ronnie blew his top.

"What do you think you're doing?", he roared, "you f******* woman!"

"Oh Ronnie!", she replied, somewhat coyly. "What a compliment! To think I could – at my age!"

Lady Mary Rose Williams

At a meet one morning Ronnie announced that a certain lady had been seen schooling a horse over a stone wall at the top of Adlestrop hill.

"She didn't think I saw her", he said, "but she'll know after the meet that I did."

He missed very little: he had to maintain discipline.

Derek Strong

35

'Ronnie would often have half the City of London behind him on a Saturday.

The finger would be crooked, and the call would come —"I want a word with so-and-so" — and you would see some frightfully important captain of industry or merchant banker spurting forward, glowing with pride in anticipation of being asked by the Master to perform some menial task.

The power of the man in his heyday was infinite. '

John Gill

'The Captain always had complete faith in his hounds, and they in him. Once, a few hounds were casting in the opposite direction to the others while trying to recover the line of a fox, and I made a move to shepherd them back.

"Leave them alone, you stupid boy!", the Captain shouted. "They're all right, you know: they've been all right for years!" '

Tony Wright

' One of his great strengths was that he was always asking people what they thought and what they'd heard. He didn't always act upon what they said, but he always listened. '

Stephen Lambert

' Ronnie Wallace was always ahead of his time. I first met him in the mid—1960's when I was beagling, and he said to me that I should be hunting hounds.

"I can't', I told him. "I haven't any money."

"The future of hunting", he said, "is people like you who've got the skill and the time, to be supported by Joint Masters who can support you financially. Those sort of people will be busy earning their money and won't have the time to run a hunt. Running hunting is going to take more and more time and has to be done more professionally if it's going to be successful."

By and large he was right, although it never quite happened like that because of inflation in the 1970's. '

Alastair Jackson

37

During a good hunt in the Evenlode Vale one day the hounds were crossing the railway line and there was a man on the line clearing vegetation and waving at us.

The Captain said, "What's that man doing?"

"He seems to be swinging his hedging hook at the hounds", I said. "He must be anti."

At that point Bill Lander turned up.

"Lander", the Captain said, "get off your horse, walk up that railway line and give that man a bloody good hiding."

With that the Captain and I moved on. Later I asked Bill what he'd done, and he said, "Waited for you two to get out of sight and then followed on quietly behind".

John Robbins

(As a corollary to this incident, Bill Lander adds, "That evening I overhead the Captain telling someone about it, and saying he was of a mind to go and sort out the man himself. Obviously he'd wanted me to soften him up first!")

Shortly after the Captain left the Heythrop we had a pair of young hounds called Farmer and Farrin — the latter named after Michael Farrin, the Quorn huntsman. I brought these two hounds out at a puppy show one day and said, "Farmer — and Michael."

A fortnight later I was at Peterborough Show when Mrs. Wills approached me, obviously upset and bearing a message from the Captain.

"It is not a good idea", she told me, "to call a hound Farrin and have the huntsman making a joke of it at a puppy show!"

Tony Collins

Ronnie was in Guiting Wood one day with John Robbins, and the hounds were really flying. They came to a bog, which threatened to hold them up, and Ronnie was impatient to keep up the pace.

"How the hell do you get out of here?", he demanded of John.

John wasn't sure, and with Ronnie champing at the bit he began to panic a little. Suddenly he said, "I know!", and rode straight through the bog and out the other side.

Nigel Peel

' Ronnie said to me many times, "The morning's for the field; the afternoon's for those of us who really appreciate hunting."

I always thought there was a tremendous difference in the afternoon. In the morning he would not be quite so particular. If he lost the line of the fox he'd move the hounds on quickly to where he knew there would be another one, and the field would think they were still hunting the same fox. But once we'd changed horses and the field was reduced it became very serious. '

Ian Alexander

' Ronnie Wallace had a particular way with hounds that no-one else could match, no matter how they tried. When Bill Lander went to hunt the Wynnstay he said, "I don't know what the bugger does. I've done the same as he did: it works for him but it doesn't work for me." '

Roger Dancer

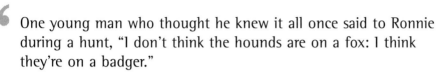

One young man who thought he knew it all once said to Ronnie during a hunt, "I don't think the hounds are on a fox: I think they're on a badger."

"I beg your pardon, sir!", Ronnie replied. "Which book did you read that in?"

Michael Clayton

The day after Harold Wilson became Prime Minister, the Captain called the second whipper-in and asked him to find Sir Hugh Donaldson, who came trotting up.

"Morning Ronnie", he said.

"Morning Hugh", the Captain replied. "This bloody Wilson - who is he?"

Bill Lander

' I was out with the Cotswold once when I was very young, and a mist came down and I realised I was lost. I followed a track, feeling very wet and cold and sorry for myself, and then the mist lifted a little and I saw a clump of trees in a walled field.

Suddenly a fox came over the wall and went into the trees, and then the hounds arrived, followed by Ronnie. I thought I'd better tell him where the fox had gone, so I kicked my pony forward.

"Stand still, you bloody stupid little girl!", Ronnie shouted.

Then the whip arrived and Ronnie said, "Just go and ask that little girl whether she's seen the fox."

I told them where it had gone and they caught it, and Ronnie said, "Now, where's that clever little girl?" '

Sandra Loder

❛ He knew where the fox was going before the fox even went there. ❜

Tom Clifford

❛ His method of handling the hounds was to be quiet, not to interfere until he had to, but when he did he did it very quickly indeed.

He had the added bonus of having a natural flair for it - what he would call woodcraft — a certain native cunning, of knowing how a fox would think. He read the signs of the countryside, automatically looking at the wind, and the behaviour of birds and other animals. ❜

Alastair Jackson

‘ A well–known racehorse trainer, renowned for his forthright speech, once saw the Heythrop crossing his gallops. Later on he telephoned the Captain and complained about this in his usual direct manner.

The Captain was unmoved. "If you want to train racehorses", he said, "go and do it somewhere else." ’

Anthony Adams

It was a very rare thing for anyone else to hunt the Heythrop hounds in the Captain's day. We were at Swinbrook once, and the only horse allowed into the covert was his horse. It was quiet, it was raining, and I couldn't hear much. Then Colonel Chamberlayne came galloping up.

"Collins", he said, "the Captain wants you".

I went into the covert and found that the Captain had run a blackthorn into his eye.

"You'll have to carry on", he told me. "If I were you I'd go in there, but go on foot." With that he announced he was off to hospital to have his eye seen to.

I went into the covert and blew on the horn, but it made a strange sound and I noticed there was a crack in it. I tried to close it up but only succeeded in breaking the horn in half. Someone realised there was a problem and went along all the cars, but all they could come up with was a kiddies' trumpet!

In the meantime Colonel Chamberlayne had gone off and found the Captain and came back with his horn. I noticed from the engraving that he'd won it at Peterborough Show, so I took good care of it.

We hunted round for about half an hour, lost the fox, and then we heard the Captain's holloa - he'd seen it. He hadn't gone off to hospital at all: he was hanging about to see how I got on!

Tony Collins

45

‘ Ronnie didn't mind what he said to anybody out hunting. I remember a frightfully smart young man coming down from Leicestershire to hunt with us. We got to the first field and we knew that for some reason we were absolutely not allowed into the field beyond it. But this young man jumped into it anyway, showing off, and Ronnie sent him home.

Afterwards he said, "Well, I couldn't not have sent him home after he did that. If it was the Prime Minister I'd have sent him home." ’

Caroline Brooks

‘ I had a chestnut mare called Kate, which I'd brought from the Oakley. She was a lovely horse, but she hated cars, and always lashed out at them. She also had huge hooves.

We were on the Oddington to Broadwell road, and we'd been pestered all day by a group of anti's who were now following us in their cars. Ronnie crooked his finger in the usual way and summoned me to his side.

"I think it might be useful if you go to the back of the field for a bit", he said.

I did so, and Ronnie suddenly stopped for no apparent reason. The whole field concertinaed behind him, the anti's car closed up behind me, and Kate kicked out furiously and made an awful mess of the front headlights and radiator. Ronnie once again demonstrated his capacity for never missing a trick. ’

Ian Alexander

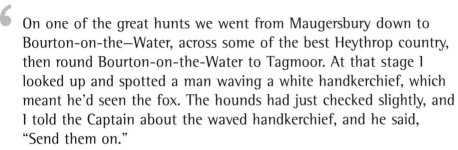

On one of the great hunts we went from Maugersbury down to Bourton-on-the–Water, across some of the best Heythrop country, then round Bourton-on-the-Water to Tagmoor. At that stage I looked up and spotted a man waving a white handkerchief, which meant he'd seen the fox. The hounds had just checked slightly, and I told the Captain about the waved handkerchief, and he said, "Send them on."

I undid the gate and went on, and as I did so another man came running down the field.

"That's not your hunted fox sir", he said.

The Captain stuck his spurs in, the horse shot forward, the hounds hit the line and he shouted, "Well it bloody soon will be!"

John Robbins

A day with the Heythrop at its height was a complete theatre production. Every detail was right. I very much doubt that we shall see again fox-hunting organised to such a high level. It was magnificent sport.

Stephen Lambert

47

' I used to train showjumping horses and often rode them out hunting. I was asked to go on to open a gate one day, and as I approached it the horse, being a showjumper, automatically tried to jump it. The ground was very boggy, however, and the horse turned a somersault and landed on top of me, crushing my ribs.

As I lay in the mud, desparately trying to breathe, I saw Dermot Daly approaching.

"Help!", I gasped.

"I can't", he said as he cantered past, "Ronnie's told me to go on to the corner."

He wasn't known as "God" for nothing. '

Lady Mary Rose Williams

'He thought like the fox.'

Mary Studd

We used to walk puppies for the Heythrop, and my youngest son was on his pony one day, going up a field with his mother. They got to a gate, and my son turned round and said, "Come along mum! I'm Captain Wallace: open the gate!"

Derek Strong

' We were hunting by Fyfield one day, the hounds had just found, and we came to a tall fence, which the Captain was never too fond of. He said to me, "Jump the fence and stop on the other side. I shall probably fall off. Catch my horse and we'll get going again."

  Which is exactly what happened. He fell off, I caught his horse, we remounted and were gone down the Gawcombe Vale before two hundred other people arrived to see what had occurred. '

John Robbins

6 We were hunting in Tangley Woods one day and I was sent out on point. I sat in a wood for ages, and then heard the hounds, who appeared to be right on the other side of the wood.

I realised I was in the wrong place, which wouldn't make me very popular, so I started off through the wood and had reached a junction with a right–angled ride when I suddenly saw Ronnie's cap. I turned round hurriedly and got behind a big oak tree. There was another ride that went off left–handed and I thought he'd probably go down that, but he turned round towards me.

Luckily the hounds were to his right and he was watching them, so he didn't see me, and eventually trotted off along another ride. It was the only time I ever fooled him: you didn't often get away with anything. 9

Derek Strong

6 He never forgot a face. He never said good morning to anyone at the meets, and out hunting, you might not see him all day. But he saw you. 9

Rob Bartlett

' He was very good with children, especially those who might become huntsmen. After my husband died I used to go with my younger son (Charlie Brooks, the former racehorse trainer) to stay with him on Exmoor, as did Marcus Armytage and his mother.

Charlie used to say that his two heroes were Lester Piggot and Captain Wallace. I remember Charlie wearing an enormous long mackintosh one very wet day, and Ronnie looked at him and said, "You can't wear that: you look like Michael Clayton!" '

Caroline Brooks

' He was one of those people who made a completely indelible impression on your life. '

Stephen Lambert

51

' If someone dies out hunting you naturally take them home.

One day on a particularly good hunt in Heythrop country some—one sadly had a heart attack and died. This was reported to Ronnie, who hissed, "Don't tell me now – tell me later!" '

Stephen Lambert

' In 1976 I judged at my first major hound show with Ronnie. I had fallen from a young horse in the stable yard a few days previously, and cracked a rib and hurt my elbow, but I was determined not to miss it, even though I was in quite a lot of pain.

Ronnie was a very quick judge of the hounds and very decisive, and every time he wanted to point something out to me he got me by the elbow, which made the pain even worse. Ronnie was oblivious to this, of course, and as we left the ring he said to me, "Well, there we are. I hope you've learned something."

Gerald Gundry, who had been watching, came across and said, "My dear fellow, you look just like the Holy Ghost!", and got me a large drink! '

Nigel Peel

We were cub-hunting at Lyneham one autumn, and we'd been out two or three hours and had had a rather boring sort of day. I was with a chap called Tom Holt — who has subsequently died and had a big cover named after him on the Leighs estate.

I said, "Come on, Tom, let's go for a gallop over a few hedges."

Tom was dubious, because Ronnie was very strict about these things, but I said, "Come on, this is my father-in-law's farm — we'll be alright."

So off we went and had a great spin across this land —not interfering with the hunting, of course — and naturally Ronnie spotted us. He stopped the hounds, collected them together, and came over to where we were.

"We're in trouble now", Tom said.

Ronnie stopped in front of us. "Huh! You is it?", he said. "Well, I suppose I can't complain about you riding all over your father-in-law's land." And off he went again.

Ian Alexander

' Ronnie was in London once for a MFHA dinner when he bumped into a friend who told him the news that the Prince of Wales had become engaged to Lady Diana Spencer.
  "Oh good!", Ronnie replied. "Does she hunt?" '

Michael Clayton

' When I first got to know Ronnie in the mid—1960's he was at the height of his powers — the very best. He was the best at handling hounds, hunting the fox, and running the hunting country. He did it far more professionally than anyone had done in the past. He never left a stone unturned. The result was a remarkable period of fox—hunting, probably as good as has ever been seen in the British Isles. '

Alastair Jackson

During the Heythrop's annual visit to the West Country one year the Captain had a bad fall and hurt his shoulder. He completed the day in my vehicle, and I had to drive as close as possible to the hounds so he could blow his horn out of the window.

Two days later we were on the Quantocks, and Bill Lander was going to hunt the hounds there for the first time. The Captain had had a painkiller and was following us, and I wasn't riding that day, so he asked me to run the terrier.

They moved off and drew, and ran to ground on the side of a hill. I put the terrier in and dug into about five foot of bank, and when the terrier came out they went away again and I spent a few minutes filling the earth in. I caught up with them at the T–junction of a track, where the horses had checked.

Bill Lander was standing at this T–junction when the Captain came along.

"Well Lander", he said, "I should do something. I shouldn't stand there all day."

Then they hit the line off and had a good hunt, and Bill caught his first fox in the river. The Captain walked up and asked where the fox was.

"Must be in the river", Bill told him.

"You can't count a fox that you can't see", the Captain said, and he made them get in the river to find it.

So all in all Bill Lander's first day's hunting was very memorable, both for him and everyone who knew him!

John Robbins

' We met at Batsford Park one Friday in early February. It had been a very wet week, and I had asked the Captain to miss my farm if at all possible. The field numbered only about twenty, but we found quickly and away we went. We crossed the A44 by Upper Rye, went through Sezincote, up over Hans Hill to Luckley, on to Banks Fee Farm, to Fox Farm, Swell Wold, through Eyford Park, through the long plantation by Upper Slaughter and back right—handed to Eyford Knoll.

The fox was eventually killed right in the place where the Captain put his dustbins out for collection. As he gathered up the hounds to get them off the busy road he turned to me and said, "We never put a foot on your farm."

After such a fine run and considering everything else he must have had on his mind at the time, I thought his attention to this small detail was quite amazing. '

Robin Dale

We met at Long Compton once and had a very good hunt —right out to Heythrop and past the church there, and the hounds were roaring on.

I was on my father-in-law's best hunter, and we came to a flimsy hedge with a 5-strand barbed wire fence on the other side.

"Go on!", Ronnie urged me. "Jump it!"

I was scared of cutting the horse, but he jumped it well, and Ronnie promptly went through a gate a short way away. He knew where they all were.

Derek Strong

On a very good day the hounds went absolutely steaming straight through a great big cover. There was a hedge, then a field. All of a sudden Ronnie stopped the hounds in this field, turned round, went back three fields, laid them on, and off they went and caught the fox.

I couldn't understand how he had known to stop them when he did, so the following day I asked him.

"Well", he said, "they were running heel way."

Only he would have realised that. He's just a one-off.

Robin Watson

57

‘ When I was second whipper-in Roger Dancer was a scout — he was always told to go on. One day he was riding a young horse and didn't want to get too close to the hounds, in case it let fly. We got to a gate that wouldn't open, the Captain was getting impatient, and Roger was trying to explain that he was worried his horse might kick the hounds.

But the Captain just wanted the gate open — fast — so Roger jumped off and was holding his horse with one hand and trying to open the gate with the other. The inevitable happened, of course — the horse let fly and kicked one of the hounds and the Captain was furious; but in his haste to get the gate open he hadn't listened to Roger. ’

Anthony Adams

‘ John and I were riding home one day, going down a valley where in retrospect we should not have gone. The fox came straight towards us, saw us, and went off at right angles.

We knew we would be in a hot spot for heading it, but I believe that in those circumstances you have to be up front about things, so when Ronnie appeared we told him what had happened.

He swept off his hat in a very theatrical gesture and said, "How very lucky you were here to see it go!" ’

Liz Wills

58

On Sundays during the summer the Captain used to bring a few people over to the kennels to look at the young hounds, and always pointed a few out. On one occasion I produced a pair called Ferneley and Fracas.

"Ferneley", I said, "and Fracass" — pronouncing the S.

The Captain walked over slowly, stood beside me, and said quietly, "Fracarr".

Tony Collins

Last year I was badly hurt out hunting, and when Ronnie heard about it he sent me the following fax:

"Many years ago a great professional told me that there were no marks for a huntsman on the ground. I have never seen a truly skilled huntsman who was always in a hurry. Do please go carefully."

Marty Wood

‘ Soon after I bought Kirkham Farm the hounds came through a cover which was pretty thick and almost impassable. Half an hour later a message came down through the field summoning me to go and see Ronnie.

"Those rides in your cover need trimming out", he said.

"Yes, they probably do", I replied, not wanting to cow-tow completely.

About a month later I had some spare time so I went round the cover with a crawler tractor and opened up every ride very thoroughly, and the next time the hounds were there they went through it like a knife through butter. I was summoned again.

"Why did you clear out all those rides your cover?", Ronnie asked me.

"I thought you would want them cleared", was the only reply I could think of. ’

John Wills

60

❛ We were crossing my step-father's farm near Chasleton one day and came to the boundary fence, which was a big obstacle with a bog on either side of it. I was riding a young horse and I pulled up to look for somewhere else to get across it.

"For God's sake get over that fence!", Ronnie grumbled, so I had a crack at it and the horse fell − straight into the gap it had made. It was lying on its side on top of me, blocking the gap, and I was soaking wet and eating clods of earth.

"Get the bloody hell out of the way!", Ronnie shouted. "What *do* you think you're doing?"

It took me about five minutes to sort myself out, with Ronnie muttering and cursing. He then expressed due gratitude to me for making a hole big enough for him to pass through. ❜

Anthony Welton

'We had a terrierman called Roger, who was a great success, but a strong character like Ronnie. Out cub-hunting on a blustery October day, a fox came out of a cover and ran past him.

"Where's it gone?", Ronnie shouted, and Roger shouted back to tell him.

"Speak up!", Ronnie shouted, "I can't hear you."

Roger tried again but Ronnie still couldn't hear him because of the wind, so Roger bellowed at the top of his voice.

"Don't you shout at me, you bloody boy!", Ronnie yelled. "If you shout at me you'll go home!"'

Stephen Lambert

'People have always said that if Ronnie hadn't been involved in fox-hunting he would have gone into politics; perhaps even become Prime Minister. I had never heard his own views on this, and at dinner one night I asked him what he would do if he had his life over again. His reply surprised me.

"I would go into the Church", he said.'

Lady Mary Rose Williams

❛ Ronnie always said that almost more important than the breeding of a foxhound was the breeding of its breeder. ❜

Alastair Jackson

❛ During my third year with the Heythrop we had hardpad among the young hounds. There were more going down every day and Tom, the kennelman, and I looked after them. It took six weeks to clear up and I had no hunting during that period.

When I went back to my first meet everyone was asking after my health and enquiring if I was better. I realised that the Captain hadn't told anyone about the distemper, in case they didn't want the hounds over their land! ❜

Bill Lander

> I was once asked to clip one of the Captain's horses, and I tied it to an old garage door while I did the job. Suddenly the horse took fright and bolted, taking the door with it, and shot through the stable yard and into the lane.
>
> There, it came across a parked car, which it failed to negotiate successfully, landing on the bonnet and causing considerable damage. Fortunately the horse itself was unharmed, and when I caught it and led it back to the yard the Captain agreed to go and see the owner of the car.
>
> The owner ranted on about loose horses, and the fact that his car was a write-off, and when he had finished the Captain calmly put his hand through the broken windscreen, pressed the horn, and said, "Well, that still works."
>
> All he said to me later was that in future I should perhaps tie the horse up to something other than a garage door.

Tony Wright

' No–one escaped his wrath. On one occasion Pat Dennis and
Brigadier Roscoe Harvey turned up to a meet after a terrific party
the night before, dressed as Tweedledum and Tweedledee. Ronnie
was not at all amused, and said so in no uncertain terms. '

Sandra Loder

'My Uncle John was riding across the Netherworton Vale one day, thinking how marvellous it all looked, with the new hunt jumps and two bridges he'd just put in. He was feeling very pleased with himself.

Ronnie called him over and Uncle John went up, thinking he was about to be congratulated for his efforts. They rode towards a well-known cover called Hawk Hill, which Uncle John had cleared and replanted.

"What have you done to Hawk Hill, John?", Ronnie said. "It's not a bloody arboretum!" '

Sandra Loder

‘ I was out cub-hunting one day with a horse that for some reason wouldn't jump ditches. We came to some big ditches on the way back and after a lot of effort and some rather vigorous encouragement I eventually got this horse to jump them.

Lavinia Jenkinson was organising the fencing at the time and she must have seen me, because I was summoned to go and see the Captain the following day. I had a severe reprimand about the way I'd treated this horse: it was like going in front of the headmaster. ’

Richard Sumner

‘ One year I was invited to judge a horn blowing competition in Churchill with the Captain. We sat in another room, as one does, and I said, "I'm not a great connoisseur, but I know that when you blow "away" it sends a shiver down my spine."

"Well then", the Captain replied, "the more your back shakes the higher the marks we'll give 'em." ’

John Robbins

67

6 I remember the day I got my hunt buttons. I kept my horses with Frank Slatter in Kingham at the time, and I was having a drink with him when Ronnie came in.

"I think you'd better get a different coloured coat for next week", he said to me quietly.

"What do you mean?", I asked him.

"I've − er − asked the secretary to let you have some buttons", he replied.

He said it in a very charming way, which made me feel extremely proud. 9

Ian Alexander

6 Ronnie is a great mixture. He could be very fierce out
hunting, but he's an extremely kind man too. Very
thoughtful. One lady member described him as being
"a devil on a horse but a darling on his feet."
  Of course we all got shouted at — individually or
collectively — at one time or another. If you found
yourself sitting next to him at dinner you half
expected him to say, "pass the salt, damn you, and
hurry up about it!", but of course he didn't: he was
absolutely charming. 9

Caroline Brooks

' I once rented some land at Dean Manor. It came on the market, and I asked the agents if I should remove my stock, but they said everything was fine, and to leave it there.

There was so much interest in the land that it went to auction, and not long after it was sold I received a letter from the new owner's solicitors requesting me to vacate the fields within Forty-eight hours.

This put me in a spot, but I remembered that Ronnie had once asked me if everything was alright with this land and told me to let him know if ever there was a problem. So I telephoned him to explain the situation.

"Leave it to me", he said.

That same evening I had a telephone call from the new owner, telling me to carry on as usual. Ronnie had been in touch with her! '

Tom Clifford

Before the start of each season Ronnie would take out a huge number of hounds for exercise. He would take young ones with older ones through large flocks of sheep, and if he saw just one hound stop and look at a sheep he would go up to it and tick it off like a child. He never belted them, only talked, and his methods worked.

Michael Clayton

I saw Ronnie come up against a big fence once and have two or three rather public refusals. As he turned round he spotted the local timber merchant coming along the ride.

"Come on!", he shouted. "You're a timber man. Come and get this fence down for me!"

Liz Wills

71

'When we first started to hunt with the Heyhtrop my brother Henry and I were known as Hammer and Tongs, presumably because of our exhuberent riding style. It was also said of us by Ronnie that one was nice and one was very nice, although we never discovered which was which. I like to think that I was the 'very nice' one, because I had a rich wife, but sadly she left me!'

John Gill

There was a lady called Iris Joy who hunted with us. She was terribly nice but almost stone deaf, so she hardly ever heard anything anyone said.

She had committed some misdemeanor one day and Ronnie, who must have been in a bad temper, absolutely let rip at her, using every swearword in the book. When he had finally run out of invective Iris turned to the rest of the field, smiled sweetly, and said, "Was he talking to me?"

Lady Mary Rose Williams

I first met Ronnie when he came to Canada to judge at the Canada Hound Show at London, Ontario. As his co-judge I was sent to meet him.

"Captain Wallace, you don't know me", I said, introducing myself. "Can I get you anything?"

"I'd like a very dry martini, please", he replied. We have been firm friends ever since.

Marty Wood

73

The Captain hardly even missed a day's hunting. A guest said to Bill Lander once, "I expect you've hunted them, have you?"

"No sir, I haven't", Bill said.

"Not even when the Captain's ill?"

"Ill?", Bill snorted. ""I've never even heard the bugger cough!"

Roger Dancer

When Sybil Roley was Master of the Ledbury she and her kennel huntsman were guests of the Heythrop one day. Hearing Ronnie blow his horn, she asked her huntsman what exactly it was he was blowing.

The man shrugged. "You can never be sure with these amateurs, madam", he replied.

Lady Mary Rose Williams

We had a huge joint meet with the Cotswold once at Batsford Park — two hundred and fifty to three hundred people. The hounds didn't find until about two o'clock, and we ran from Bourton-on-the-Hill to Broadwell and straight through Moreton-in-Marsh and back round, and lost the fox by the railway line.

I was going through Moreton flat out when I saw the Captain trotting quietly over the railway bridge. I thought, "where are you going?", but the fox was there and the Captain was in the right place at the right time. He had a sixth sense.

Robin Dale

❝ He's two personalities. He's probably the best host you could ever have - charming and thoughtful and witty. But on the hunting field he's a general. ❞

Robin Watson

❝ We met for cub-hunting one hot autumn day and sat waiting for about half an hour. The horses were defecating and the flies were busy. Eventually the Captain arrived and everybody squared up.

"Oh look!", one of the lady members said, "everyone's moved."

"Yes", Anthony Adams muttered, "even the bloody flies have moved!" ❞

Tony Collins

'When I was in my teens in my early years with the Heythrop Ronnie was very understanding of our age—group. He knew that we liked to gallop about and jump a lot, which in many ways was anathema to him because he was such a purist.

He once called at our house for tea after hunting, and said to me, "I'm sorry we didn't get in the Vale for you today. You didn't get enough jumping." '

Anthony Welton

'The Captain and I were sat on our horses at the end of a good day's cub-hunting round Guiting Hill. We'd been round the North Cots and we'd cut a few gaps in the wire here and there so the Captain could get about.

"Well", he said, "we've had a very good morning: we've opened up the North Cotswold country." '

John Robbins

77

'He didn't have much time for women unless he thought they could be of some use to him. He once rang me up and said, "Sandra, would you happen to be at home tomorrow? I'd just like to come and see you."

"Can't you tell me over the phone?", I said.

"Well", he replied, "I'd just like to come and see you"

"Ronnie", I told him, "whatever it is, the answer is no."

He arrived anyway, and it turned out to be something to do with the British Field Sports Society. '

Sandra Loder

'I remember an occasion in early November when he gave Bill Lander the most tremendous dressing down in front of everyone. Bill took it, and when the Captain had moved on he said to the rest of us, "I thought it was firework night last night, but it seems that one or two haven't gone off yet!"'

Anthony Adams

'In his last few years at the Heythrop Ronnie didn't jump many fences, preferring to proceed quietly through gates whenever possible. The late Tom Holt, who was known as a bit of a thruster, saw him approaching a gate one day and rushed to open it. Ronnie pointedly ignored him, and jumped the fence.'

Sally Gill

'After a morning's cub–hunting we eventually caught the fox and I was told to get it out of the ditch. It was a very deep ditch, and I'm not very tall, and I handed the fox up to Ronnie and then put up my hand to get a lift out of the ditch myself. He completely ignored me, turned round and walked away!'

Nigel Peel

' One day the hunted fox somehow got itself into a supermarket in Chipping Norton, where needless to say it caused considerable consternation amoung the customers and staff.

It was obvious that someone would have to go into the store and sort things out, and we were all busy trying to make ourselves invisible when the Captain turned to me.

"I think you'd better go in there", he said. "I don't know very much about these places."

I had no choice of course, and I managed to defuse what could have been an embarrassing public relations disaster; but what the Captain didn't realise was that I never went shopping myself. I didn't know very much about the store either, or the people in it. '

Tony Collins

81

6 I was cub-hunting with Ronnie on Exmoor once when I saw a single hound half-heartedly chasing a sheep. Ronnie waved his arms, a man in a car some distance away waved back, and the hound was caught and taken off. I asked what would happen to it now.

"Oh, he'll go to a country with no sheep", Ronnie told me.

He expected the same high standard from his hounds as he did from humans. 9

Daphne Flowers Wood

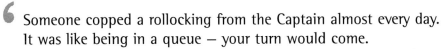

' Someone copped a rollocking from the Captain almost every day. It was like being in a queue – your turn would come.

He called Richard Sumner up to the head of the field one day. When Richard came back he said that the Captain had told him he had done something incorrectly, but Richard maintained he was right, and said so.

"Well, you're in the wrong now", the Captain replied, "because you're arguing with me!" '

Bill Lander

' He was immensely generous with his time. He would go anywhere to help a little pack of hounds, and do anything he could to encourage them. He takes immense trouble with people. '

Stephen Lambert

6 When the Captain gave you a serious rollocking out hunting you'd learn something if you bothered to sort it out. Sometimes you'd laugh, but I was told it was nothing to grin at.

The first time he ever gave me a roasting was in my first season. We were cub-hunting, and had got to a place where there were foxes going all ways. I could see that the hounds might be running heel, so I prepared myself for that. He was shouting and hollering at me to do what I was going to do anyway, so I was grinning.

We caught the fox, had a long hack back, and we were trotting along with all the ladies and gentlemen behind us, including the Duke of Marlborough. The Captain crooked his finger at me in that way of his, meaning "come here", and I went trotting up.

"Collins", he said, "you mustn't keep grinning when I'm telling you these things. You must realise that there's people go out hunting who hoot and halloa; they crack whips; they blow hunting horns. They know nothing about it. I'm trying to teach you the proper way." 9

Tony Collins

'When Bob Johnson kept the Fosse Manor Hotel just outside Stow-on-the-Wold we often went there for a drink in the evening after hunting. I remember Ronnie turning up on one occasion, still in his hunting clothes, having obviously visited a few farmers.

He stood in front of the fire with a glass in his hand and began to talk about the day's hunting. The rest of us sat there for two hours, just listening. He was absolutely riveting: he could remember every detail of the day, and he knew exactly which hound had done what. '

Ian Alexander

‘ During a huge meet at Eyford, when I'd just come from the North Cotswold, I went to undo a gate and found I hadn't got a knife with me. The hounds were running and the Captain got in a temper as I fumbled with the string.

"North Cots person, not properly dressed, no bloody penknife!", he growled, and he gave his horse such a crack that my horse shot across the next cornfield and I had to run to fetch it.

As a consequence, the last thing I always look for when I go hunting is a penknife, even to this day. ’

John Robbins

‘ I was with him for seven seasons, and I don't suppose he came on hound exercise with me in the summer more than half a dozen times. But when the season started he would come to the kennels on the first morning and although they'd hardly seen him all summer they immediately flocked around him. He just had that way with them. ’

Tony Collins

❛ Tony Collins and I were sat round a cover one day when we really shouldn't have been there. Eventually we caught the field up and slipped in, but of course the Captain had spotted us.

"You two are like a pair of bloody cream puffs!", he said. ❜

Anthony Adams

❛ In the late 1950's and 1960's the Peterborough championship became known as the battle of the green coats — Ronnie versus the Duke of Beaufort. They were both ultra-competitive, but Ronnie managed to hide his feelings, whereas the Duke did not.

The first time I judged at Peterborough was with Bob Field-Marsham, Master of the Eridge Hounds. We gave it to the Heythrop, and Bob advised me to avoid the Duke for the next couple of hours. He was right: I bumped into the Duke in the gents and he was not in the best of tempers. ❜

Alastair Jackson

In Heythrop country he would talk to anyone who could be useful, from wealthy landowners to
publicans. At one stage he became very friendly with the manager of a sewage farm, because he knew the foxes tended to go there, and he was also on good terms with the people at a fire station, which had a lot of grass around it where the foxes would lie up. All this was part of his preparation for hunting days to come.

Michael Clayton

We were standing on the railway line in the Evenlode Vale one day when the hounds came past us, and as they did so one of the horses kicked out at them. Ronnie was furious, and for some reason thought that my horse was responsible.

"It wasn't me", I told him, but he was having none of it.

"Don't argue!", he said, "Go home!"

So I trotted off, not best pleased at being the victim of an injustice, and a little while later the whipper-in came galloping after me.

"Lady Mary", he called, "you can come back. Someone else has confessed."

I went back, of course.

Lady Mary Rose Williams

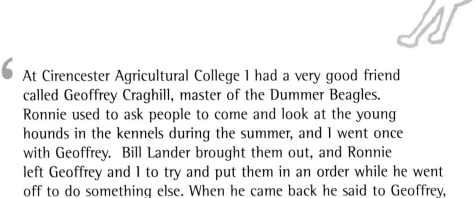

At Cirencester Agricultural College I had a very good friend called Geoffrey Craghill, master of the Dummer Beagles. Ronnie used to ask people to come and look at the young hounds in the kennels during the summer, and I went once with Geoffrey. Bill Lander brought them out, and Ronnie left Geoffrey and I to try and put them in an order while he went off to do something else. When he came back he said to Geoffrey, "By Jove, you're improving! There was a time when you would have had the draft dancing about down here!"

Alastair Jackson

We were at Hyde Farm in the Lower Slaughter Vale one day. The Captain had just changed horses and I went on to get a gate open, but he went sailing over the hedge.

"I didn't realise you wanted to jump", I said, "so I opened the gate."

"I didn't want to jump", he told me. "The bloody horse bolted!"

John Robbins

89

' In 1970 the Captain was Chairman of the Master of Foxhounds Association. He told me I would be on my own a lot during that period (except for the actual hunting, of course), and he was quite happy to leave it all to me. But he did say, "You won't go to the vet's too much, will you?" '

Tony Collins

' One day I overheard Lavinia Jenkinson talking to someone who Ronnie had sent home.

"You didn't go, did you?", she said to him.

"Yes, I did", this fellow replied. "Dare I go out again?"

"Oh yes, of course!", Lavinia told him. "He'll have forgotten all about it by tonight." '

Tom Clifford

'Victor Hoare used to be our neighbour, and he had a season with the Heythrop before he gave up. He then became a typical ex–hunting gent – a bit crusty and tricky, but of course he would never try to stop it.

To his delight one year his mower killed a fox while he was hay-making. Soon after that he was at a dinner with Ronnie and he told this story not once, not twice, but several times during the course of the evening.

"Would you like the bale?", he kept asking Ronnie. '

John Wills

'He has the capacity to take great pains: he's very good at detail as well as seeing the whole picture. I hunted with him for the first time when I came up from Dorset, and at the end of the day he made sure my horse was alright - fed and watered and so on.

He was also very good with young people. He went to a lot of trouble to show them hunting. '

Michael Clayton

91

'I don't know anything about the science of hunting hounds, but I noticed on Exmoor that it isn't just hounds — it's all dogs. He had a retriever and a Peke, and they were obviously devoted to him: they did everything he said. He has this affinity with dogs of all kinds. '

Caroline Brooks

'We were with the Tiverton Hunt one day and had parked the lorry in a farmyard. As we came back the farmer was getting his cows in, so Anthony Adams got into the lorry to move it. He let the handbrake off, and the lorry rolled backwards and knocked a gate and a post clean over.

I could see that the Captain was about to go mad, but the farmer said, "That's alright, it was rotten anyway."

So the Captain didn't say another word. As long as there was no damage he was quite happy! '

John Robbins

❛ Fox—hunting would not be at the height it is now without everything he has done for it over fifty years and more. ❜

Stephen Lambert

❛ He wasn't a great horseman but he had the country built to suit him. He could jump anywhere because he'd had all the fences put right, and he always had good horses.

He also organised the country. If a big estate or farm came on the market he had a client for it before anyone else had a look-in. ❜

Roger Dancer

93

❝ Ronnie once saw someone repairing a fence in the corner of
a field.
   "Just leave a small gap at the end", he told the man, "so I know
it's there and can get through." ❞

Sandra Loder

❝ Because he was so good at both the hunting of the hounds and
the organisation of hunting, he had this extra dimension. He
controlled every aspect of the Heythrop country. ❞

Alastair Jackson

94

On my first time out with the Exmoor I was with Ronnie, and Marty, my husband, was with Tony Wright, some distance away and out of sight. I had not hunted much in England, and I'd noticed that there was not much holloaing, so when I spotted a fox I said to Ronnie, "May I give a holloa?"

"By all means go ahead", Ronnie replied, so I let go a rip-roaring South Georgia holloa.

At this point Tony turned to Marty and said, "What on earth was that?"

"My wife, I think", Marty replied.

"Sounded like a bloody Red Indian!", Tony said.

Daphne Flowers Wood

95

‘ We used to hunt next to a big farm whose owner was alright, but
he had a farm manager who thought that he owned the place and
was anti. If this chap saw us on the land he would chase after us
on his tractor.

   We came up to the farm one day and saw a sign on the
boundary railing which said "Hunt Keep Off". The Captain
immediately ordered it taken down, and someone was tugging
away at it when the tractor approached. He turned round to the
Captain for support, but suprisingly the Captain had disappeared! ’

Anthony Adams

96

On one of our annual visits to Exmoor we had spent the day with the Torrington Farmers. As we prepared to leave the Captain asked me which way I went through Barnstaple on the way back. I told him, and he explained that he knew a short cut, and that he'd wait for me at the first set of traffic lights.

He was there, and I followed him, and almost immediately he turned right into Butchers Row. It was very narrow, with blinds extending out over the shop fronts, and the Captain had failed to take into account the fact that I was driving a horsebox.

I must have taken half a dozen of these blinds down as I went along. I could see them flying about in my rearview mirror, but I just kept going! We did not use that particular short cut again.

Bill Lander

I remember a marvellous hunt on one of the Heythrop's visits to South Devon. We had a six and a half mile point in the morning, but no conclusion, then the Captain changed horses. In the afternoon we found the fox, which came out of a big dingle, but after a long time the Captain still hadn't come out himself.

I waited, and saw which way the hounds went — Anthony Adams had slipped on with them over a road — but by the time the Captain appeared the whole field had gone.

We got on and rode hard out, and had to track them, and it took us three or four miles to get them in sight and catch up. Anthony had seen the fox into some paddocks by a farm, had gone left, checked, cast them all round and thought he must have missed the fox. The Captain was very annoyed about this and had gone back to where they'd last hunted in case there was any ground they'd missed.

In the meantime I said to a man in the farmyard, "Open that chicken hut door." He did, and the fox flew out. The hounds came and did a quick circuit of the yard, the fox went into the garden, and the hounds killed it right outside the front door of the farmhouse.

The Captain knocked on the door.

"I'm awfully sorry", he said to the farmer's wife when she opened it, "we've just killed the fox on your front doorstep."

"Don't worry about that", the lady replied. "It's been taking our poultry."

The Captain looked very relieved. "In that case", he said, "could I have a glass of water and two aspirins, please."

John Robbins

'In his last season at the Heythrop the Captain produced a horse called Klondike. It was a coloured horse, and not really the thing you would expect the Master to ride. We were sat waiting for him to arrive at a meet one morning, and Anthony Adams was holding Klondike.

"Whose is that?", someone asked. "It looks like a bloody clown's horse."

"Yes", Anthony replied, "and there's a bloody clown going to get on it!"'

Tony Collins

'If the Captain asked you which way a fox had gone you would point, and naturally turn your head in the same direction, and he would shout, "Will you please look at me when I'm talking to you!"'

Anthony Adams

99

‘ We were in mid–Devon country and I was terrierman for the day. They'd run in a huge circle across Dartmoor: I'd been running on and the fox passed me, I could see the hounds so I waved my handkerchief and they flew past. One of the huntsmen said, "You can run on now: we've been six miles in a circle and the fox won't come back here".

They went to ground in some rocks and I saw two figures coming back - Bill Lander and Bernard Parker. They spotted me, and I got on Bill's horse with two terriers and a spade, which didn't leave much room for him.

"Take your foot out the stirrup", he said to Bernard, "I'm coming up behind." So the red and the green set off across Dartmoor on one horse. ’

John Robbins

‘ When Ronnie became Chairman of the MFHA he spent a massive amount of time going round the country judging puppy shows, and meeting people, and he built up an unrivalled knowledge of everyone in hunting.

He also applied his very good brain to the breeding of foxhounds, and he had a natural flair for it - like green fingers. ’

Alastair Jackson

100

❝ It was a big team thing, with a lot of like-minded people involved, and he was the leader. He had this way of doing it all correctly and politely, and you'd do it with him. But if people were taking too much for granted he'd put them in their place: he'd send them home — even take his hounds home. Right was right and it had to be done right. ❞

Robin Dale

❝ His forward thinking and meticulous organisation contributed greatly to his success. I can honestly say that during his time at the Heythrop I never experienced a dull day's hunting. ❞

Peter Pauling

' Soon after I joined the Heythrop I accompanied the Captain, Anthony Adams and Tony Collins on a round of visiting the local farmers one evening, and I was introduced to the custom of having a drink of whisky and milk.

The Captain didn't think it would be a good idea for me to imbibe at the first few stops, although he, Anthony and Tony gratefully accepted all the hospitality on offer. Bearing in mind we had left the kennels before breakfast, and had been in the saddle for hours, I was surprised at what little effect the drinks seemed to have on them. I slipped through the net at the final port of call, and although the mixture tasted awful at first, it began to slip down rather well after a few mouthfuls.

On the way home I was sure I could detect a silly grin creeping onto Anthony's face, and I myself began to giggle at any remark he made. Luckily the clip—clop of the horses hooves on the tarmac lanes prevented any of my silly noises reaching the ears of the Captain, and in the end I was just extremely relieved to get back to the stable yard without falling off. '

Tony Wright

' The Captain's ability to persuade the right people to buy land when it came up for sale was well known. I was crossing some land at Little Compton once when I came across the new owner, who was looking somewhat bemused.

"Have you seen any pheasants about?", he asked me. "The Captain told me I must buy this shoot." '

Bill Lander

' Everyone who knows him has said that Ronnie would have made a brilliant politician, and some of us used to think that if he had been in the government he might not have been Prime Minister, but definitely Foreign Secretary, because he's such a great diplomat. He's very good at wheeling and dealing behind the scenes, and getting things done. '

Caroline Brooks

103

‘ By 1970 Ronnie was concerned that the otter population was declining alarmingly, and he came to the conclusion that if a quarry is drastically diminishing you don't hunt it. Along with Marcus Kimball (now Lord Kimball) and others he made the decision to voluntarily stop otter hunting, rather than have it banned.

It was quite a decision to make, because although subsequent events have proved him right, at the time he had to persuade a lot of people that it was the best thing to do. His influence in this is not widely known, because he was largely working behind the scenes, but it was no mean feat. He was a lot more far-sighted than many people involved in the countryside at that time. ’

Michael Clayton

‘ Victor Hoare and I were watching the hunt from the top of a hill one day, and Ronnie was drawing a cover. Five or six foxes and one hare emerged, and guess what he hunted?

We looked at each other and said, "Are you going to tell him?", but neither of us dared. Two or three fields later they were put right. ’

John Wills

‘ There were times when you felt he wasn't right in what he said, but when you sat back and thought about it you could see his reasoning. ’

Richard Sumner

‘ Sheila Wilcox was a great 3-day eventer who had won Badminton and represented Great Britain at the Olympics. She hunted with us sometimes, and one day I heard the Captain say — with or without some satisfaction I could not tell - "The Union Jack's on the floor." It took me a few minutes to realise that Miss Wilcox had taken a fall. ’

John Robbins

‘ Anthony Adams and I were cub-hunting one day. We found a fox and the hounds killed it on the Bloxham to Barford road. There was no-one else about and we trotted back to where we'd come from, and news got to us that the Captain had had a fall and damaged his ribs.

Naturally we thought we'd be alright for the rest of the day, but when we reached the Captain, who was propped up in a Land Rover, he said, "I think you'd better go home now."

It was a great disappointment: we had been looking forward to a rare opportunity to hunt the hounds. ’

Tony Collins

‘ Ronnie has always been hard on his staff, but none of them regret it, I think. They learned such a lot by working with him that they were happy to put up with the retribution he dished out fairly regularly. ’

Stephen Lambert

' Ronnie has the knack of being able to persuade anyone to do anything, regardless of whether or not they actually want to do it.

I used to school his young horses and sometimes drive the horsebox for him, and once, when I had flu, my sister told me, "Whatever Ronnie says, no matter how much he begs you, you are not to drive the horsebox. You are to stay in bed."

I promised I would, but when Ronnie rang me a little later and asked me to do it, I found myself saying, 'Yes of course Ronnie." '

Lady Mary Rose Williams

' Fox-hunting may be a small world and not a commercial one, and therefore not so widely talked about except in the political context, but within that world there would be no-one who doesn't know him. He's a legend in his own lifetime. I was lucky enough to see him in his prime and to see him hunt hounds just as beautifully in his old age. '

Alastair Jackson

❛ I was with him at dinner once when he said to me. "What's going to spoil hunting in the future?"

"A Labour government, perhaps?", I suggested.

"No!", Ronnie replied emphatically. "Winter barley."

He was right. After the early 1970's we rarely jumped any walls or ran across turf. The winter countryside was transformed, and once again Ronnie had displayed his farsightedness. ❜

John Gill

    'Ronnie Wallace has been the mentor and guide to many Masters and huntsmen on both sides of the Atlantic. His maintenance of standards in fox-hunting have contributed immeasurably to the sport, and his ability to convey those standards with a firm but at the same time gentle hand will ensure that the great traditions of hunting a pack of hounds will carry on forever. '

Marty Wood

6 Ronnie Wallace is the one name in hunting that will
be most remembered, certainly this last century,
beyond any other man — master or professional
huntsman — as being head and shoulders above anyone else involved in fox—hunting. 9

Alastair Jackson

' I hunted with him for twenty-five years, and the only time I ever heard him blow for home was on his last day with the Exmoor. It brought tears to my eyes. '

Clem Barton